The tiger is a feline. This means it is a member of the cat family.

The tiger is the largest cat in the world. Including its tail, a tiger may be more than 10 feet long.

The tiger is a carnivorous
animal. This means it eats meat.

When it is fully grown, a tiger weighs
more than 600 pounds.

The tiger has yellow fur
with black stripes.

Tigers live in Asia, mostly in India.

The tiger hunts large and small animals—and sometimes people.

The tiger is a wonderful swimmer.

Tigers are often put to work in the circus.

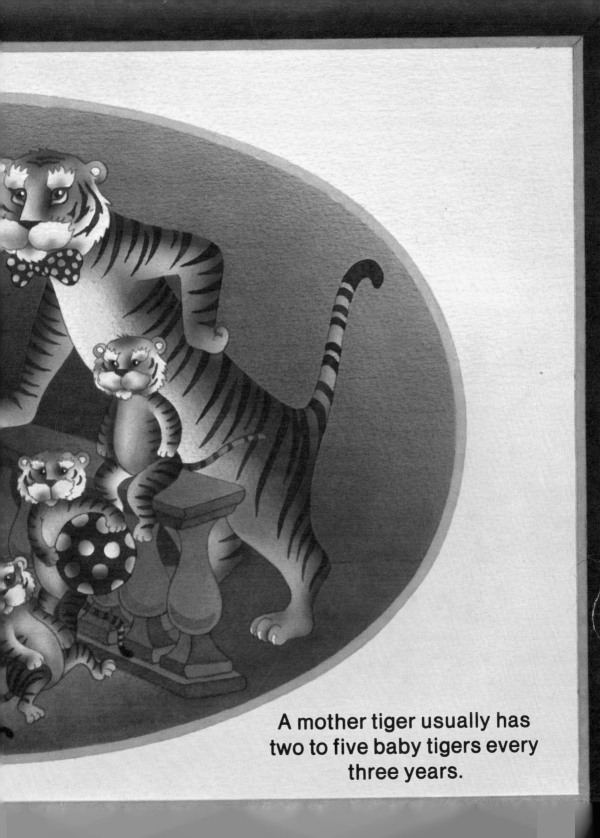

A mother tiger usually has
two to five baby tigers every
three years.